# SONGS OF England

Music arranged and processed by Barnes Music Engraving Ltd
East Sussex TN22 4HA, England

Cover design and typesetting by Paul Clark Designs

Published 1995

© International Music Publications Limited
Southend Road, Woodford Green, Essex IG8 8HN, England

# A-Roving

Traditional

2   Her eyes are like two stars so bright
Mark well what I do say!
Her eyes are like two stars so bright
Her face is fair, her step is light
I'll go no more a-roving with you, fair maid!
*A-roving, a-roving, since roving's been my ruin*
*I'll go no more a-roving with you fair maid*

3   Her cheeks are like the rosebuds red
Mark well what I do say!
Her cheeks are like the rosebuds red
There's a wealth of hair upon her head
I'll go no more a-roving with you, fair maid!
   *A-roving, a-roving, since . . .*

4   I took the maiden for a walk
Mark well what I do say!
I took the maiden for a walk
And sweet and loving was our talk
I'll go no more a-roving with you, fair maid!
   *A-roving, a-roving, since . . .*

5   I took the maiden on my knee
Mark well what I do say!
I took the maiden on my knee
She said, 'Young man, you're rather free'
I'll go no more a-roving with you, fair maid!
   *A-roving, a-roving, since . . .*

6   I put my arm around her waist
Mark well what I do say!
I put my arm around her waist
She said, 'Young man, you're in great haste'
I'll go no more a-roving with you, fair maid!
   *A-roving, a-roving, since . . .*

7   I love this fair maid as my life
Mark well what I do say!
I love this fair maid as my life
And soon she'll be my little wife
I'll go no more a-roving with you, fair maid!
   *A-roving, a-roving, since . . .*

8   And if you'd know this maiden's name
Mark well what I do say!
And if you'd know this maiden's name
Why soon like mine, 'twill be the same
I'll go no more a-roving with you fair maid!
   *A-roving, a-roving, since . . .*

# Barbara Allen

Traditional

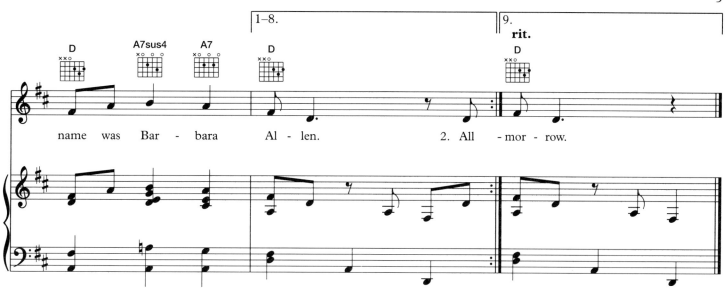

name was Bar - bara Al - len.                2. All                -mor - row.

2  All in the merry month of May
   When the green buds were swelling
   Sweet William came from the western states
   And he courted Barbara Allen

3  It was all in the month of June
   When things were all a-blooming
   Sweet William on his death-bed lay
   For the love of Barbara Allen

4  He sent his servants to the town
   Where Barbara was a-dwelling
   My master is sick and sends for you
   If your name be Barbara Allen

5  So slowly, slowly she arose
   She went and soon came nigh him
   And all she said when she got there
   Was 'Young man, I think you're dying'

6  Oh yes, he said I'm very sick
   And death is on me dwelling
   No better, no better can I ever be
   If I can't have Barbara Allen

7  As she was walking o'er the fields
   She heard the death bell knelling
   And every stroke did seem to say
   You hard-hearted Barbara Allen

8  Oh mother, oh mother, make my bed
   Go make it long and narrow
   Sweet William died for pure, pure love
   And I shall die for sorrow

9  Oh father, oh father, dig me my grave
   Go dig it long and narrow
   Sweet William died for me today
   I'll die for him tomorrow

# Blow Away The Morning Dew

Traditional

1. There was a farm-er's son, kept sheep all on the hill, and

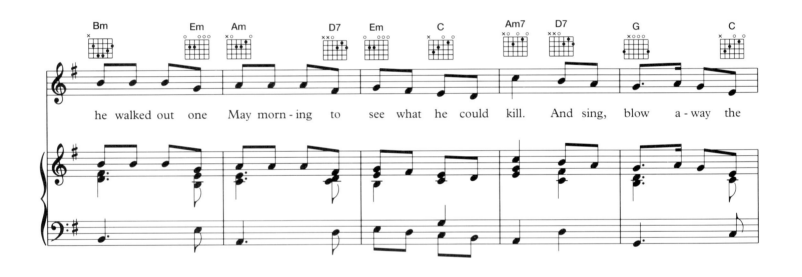

he walked out one May morn-ing to see what he could kill. And sing, blow a-way the

morn-ing dew, the dew and the dew, oh blow a-way the morn-ing dew, how

2   He looked high, he looked low
    He cast an under look
    And there he saw a fair pretty maid
    Beside the watery brook
        *And sing, blow away the morning dew*
        *The dew and the dew*
        *Blow away the morning dew*
        *How sweet the winds do blow*

3   Cast over me my mantle fair
    And pin it o'er my gown
    And if you will take hold my hand
    And I will be your own
        *And sing, blow away . . .*

4   If you come down to my father's house
    Which is walled all around
    Then you shall have my maidenhead
    And twenty thousand pounds
        *And sing, blow away . . .*

5   He mounted on a milk-white steed
    And she upon another
    And then they rode upon the lane
    Like sister and like brother
        *And sing, blow away . . .*

6   As they were riding on alone
    They saw some pooks of hay
    Oh, is this not a pretty place
    For girls and boys to play?
        *And sing, blow away . . .*

7   But when they came to her father's gate
    So nimble she popped in
    And said 'There is a fool without
    And here's a maid within'
        *And sing, blow away . . .*

8   And if you meet a lady gay
    As you go by the hill
    And if you will not when you may
    You shall not when you will
        *And sing, blow away . . .*

# Blow The Man Down

Traditional

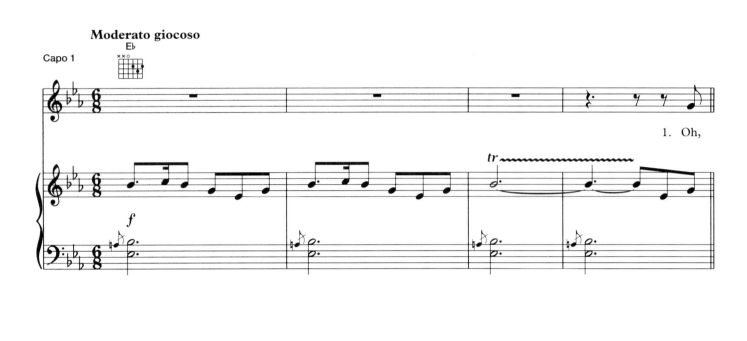

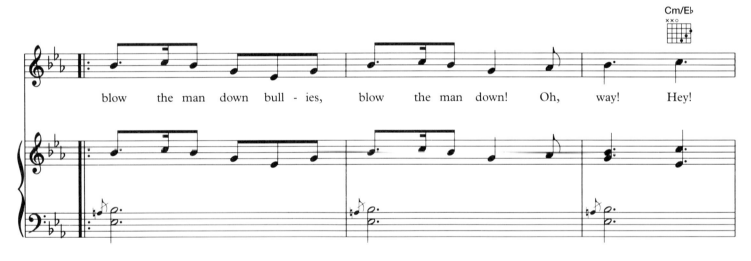

blow the man down bull - ies, blow the man down! Oh, way! Hey!

Blow the man down. Oh, blow the man down bull - ies, blow the man down, oh,

give me some time to blow the man down!

1–6.　　　　　　　　　　　7.

2. As

2　As I was a-walking down Paradise Street
　　Oh way! Hey! Blow the man down
　　A pretty young damsel I happened to meet
　　She had a man, oh blow the man down

3　I hailed her in English, she answered me clear
　　Oh way! Hey! Blow the man down
　　I took the suggestion and I had no fear
　　Give me some time to blow the man down

4　I swung to the left and I swung to the right
　　Oh way! Hey! Blow the man down
　　But he was a guy who sure knew how to fight
　　Give me some time to blow the man down

5　Guess I had one too many with pals at the bar
　　Oh way! Hey! Blow the man down
　　Or else I'd be certain to lick him by far
　　Give me some time to blow the man down

6　The adorable damsel, when she saw me fall
　　Oh way! Hey! Blow the man down
　　Took off with her hero so handsome and tall
　　Give me some time to blow the man down

7　All ye sailors take warning before you set sail
　　Oh way! Hey! Blow the man down
　　If he's strong as an ox and as big as a whale
　　Think twice before you blow the man down

# The British Grenadiers

Traditional

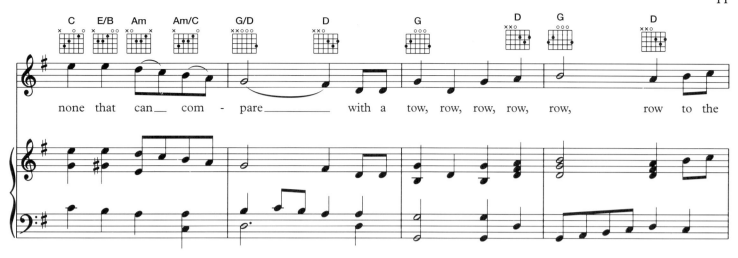

none that can\_ com - pare_____ with a tow, row, row, row, row, row to the

Bri - tish Gre - na - diers. 2. None Bri - tish Gre - na - diers.

2   None of those ancient heroes
      E'er saw a cannon ball
      Or knew the force of powder
      To slay their foes withal
      But our brave boys do know it
      And banish all their fears
      Singing tow row row row row row
      To the British Grenadiers

3   Then let us fill a bumper
      And drink a health to those
      Who carry caps and pouches
      And wear the loopèd clothes
      May they and their commanders
      Live happy all their years
      With a tow row row row row row
      To the British Grenadiers

# Charlie Mopps

Traditional

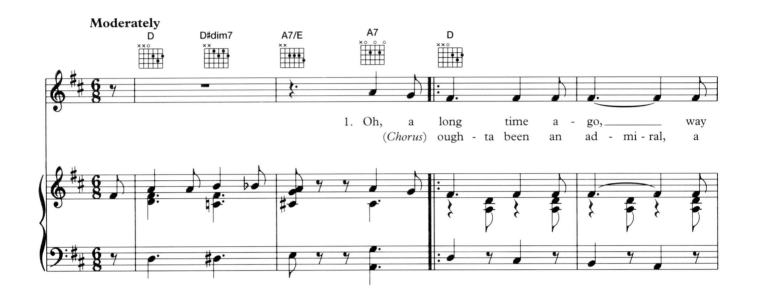

1. Oh, a long time a-go,_____ way
(*Chorus*) ough-ta been an ad-mi-ral, a

back in his-to-ry,_____ when all they had to drink was
sul-tan or a king,_____ and to his prais-es

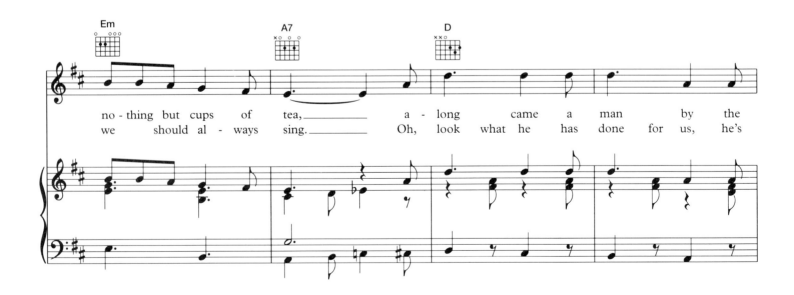

no-thing but cups of tea,_____ a-long came a man by the
we should al-ways sing._____ Oh, look what he has done for us, he's

name of Char - lie Mopps,_____ and he in - vent - ed a won - der - ful drink, and he
filled us up with cheer,_____ Lord bless Char - lie Mopps, the

gave it the name of hops. *Chorus* Oh, he beer, beer. beer, did - dle - y.
man who in - vent - ed

*last time repeat and fade*

2    The Abbey, The Connaught, The Hole In The Wall as well
        One thing you can be sure, it's Charlie's beer they sell
        So come on all you lucky lads, at ten o'clock she stops
        For five short seconds remember Charlie Mopps
        (*spoken*) One . . . two . . . three . . . four . . . five . . .
           *Oh he oughta been an admiral, a sultan or a king*
           *And to his praises we should always sing*
           *Oh look what he has done for us, he's filled us up with cheer*
           *Lord bless Charlie Mopps, the man who invented beer*

3    A bushel of hops and a barrel of malt and stir around with a stick
        The sort of lubrication to make your engine tick
        Twenty pints of wallop a day will keep away the quacks
        It's only fourpence ha'penny a pint and a shilling and tuppence in tax
        (*spoken*) Shame . . . shame . . . shame . . .
           *Oh he oughta been an admiral . . .*

# Drink To Me Only With Thine Eyes

Words by Ben Johnson
Music Traditional

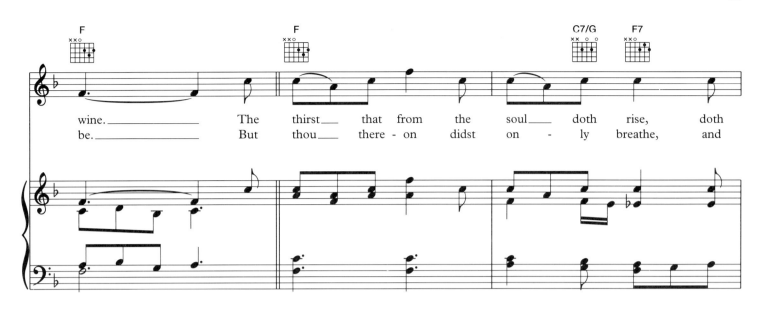

The thirst___ that from the soul___ doth rise, doth
But thou___ there - on didst on - ly breathe, and

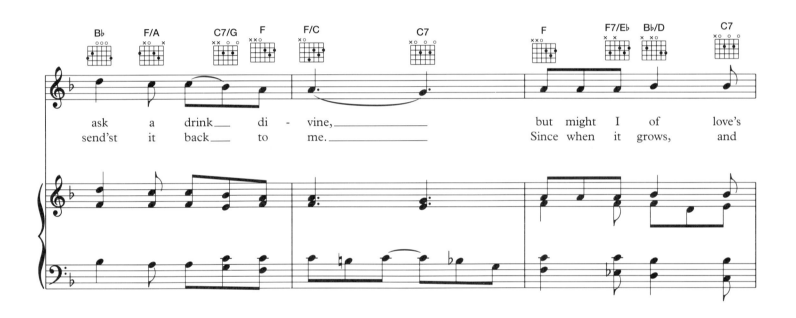

ask a drink___ di - vine,_____ but might I of love's
send'st it back___ to me._____ Since when it grows, and

nec - tar sip,___ I would___ not change for thine.
smells,___ I swear,___ not of___ it - self, but thee.

# Early One Morning

Traditional

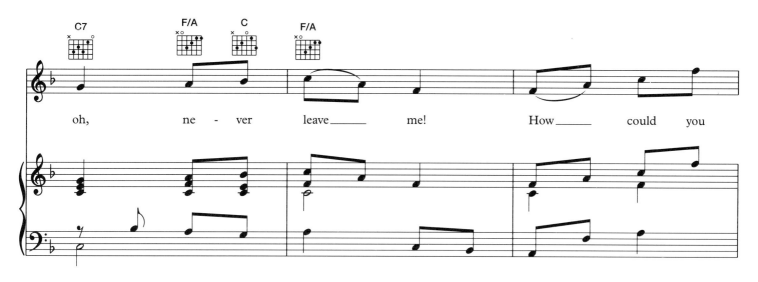

oh, ne - ver leave____ me! How____ could you

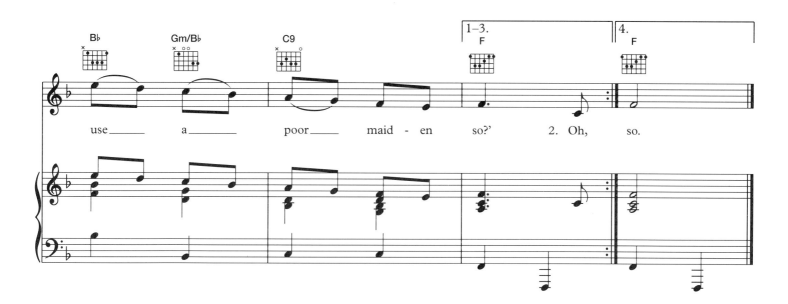

use____ a____ poor____ maid - en so?' 2. Oh, so.

2 Oh, gay is the garland and fresh are the flowers
I've culled from the garden to bind on thy brow
'Oh, don't deceive me, oh, never leave me!
How could you use a poor maiden so?'

3 Remember remember the vows you made to Mary
Remember remember you vowed to be true
'Oh, don't deceive me, oh, never leave me!
How could you use a poor maiden so?'

4 Thus sang the poor maiden, her sorrows bewailing
Thus sang the poor maiden in the valley below
'Oh, don't deceive me, oh, never leave me!
How could you use a poor maiden so?'

# The Foggy Foggy Dew

Traditional

2  One night she knelt close by my side
   As I lay fast asleep
   She threw her arms around my neck
   And then began to weep
   She wept she cried she tore her hair
   Ah me, what could I do?
   So all night long I held her in my arms
   Just to keep her from the foggy foggy dew

3  Oh I am a bachelor, I live with my son
   We work at the weaver's trade
   And every single time I look into his eyes
   He reminds me of the fair young maid
   He reminds me of the winter time
   And of the summer too
   And the many many times I held her in my arms
   Just to keep her from the foggy foggy dew

# Froggie Went A-Courting

Traditional

2 He rode up to Miss Mousie's door
A hum, a hum
He rode up to Miss Mousie's door
Where he had often been before
A hum, a hum

3 He said, 'Miss Mouse, are you within?'
A hum, a hum
He said, 'Miss Mouse, are you within?'
'Just lift the latch and please come in'
A hum, a hum

4 He took Miss Mousie on his knee
A hum, a hum
He took Miss Mousie on his knee
And said, 'Miss Mousie, will you marry me?'
A hum, a hum

5 'Without my Uncle Rat's consent?'
A hum, a hum
'Without my Uncle Rat's consent
I would not marry the president'
A hum, a hum

6 Now Uncle Rat, when he came home
A hum, a hum
Now Uncle Rat, when he came home
Said 'Who's been here since I've been gone?'
A hum, a hum

7 'A very fine gentleman has been here'
A hum, a hum
'A very fine gentleman has been here
Who wishes me to be his dear'
A hum, a hum

8 Then Uncle Rat laughed and shook his sides
A hum, a hum
Then Uncle Rat laughed and shook his sides
To think his niece would be a bride
A hum, a hum

9 So Uncle Rat, he went to town
A hum, a hum
Uncle Rat, he went to town
To buy his niece a wedding gown
A hum, a hum

10 Where will the wedding breakfast be?
A hum, a hum
Where will the wedding breakfast be?
Away down yonder in the hollow tree
A hum, a hum

11 What will the wedding breakfast be?
A hum, a hum
What will the wedding breakfast be?
Two green beans and a black-eyed pea
A hum, a hum

12 The first to come was the bumblebee
A hum, a hum
The first to come was the bumblebee
He danced a jig with Miss Mousie
A hum, a hum

13 The next to come was Mister Drake
A hum, a hum
The next to come was Mister Drake
He ate up all of the wedding cake
A hum, a hum

14 They all went sailing on the lake
A hum, a hum
They all went sailing on the lake
And they all got swallowed by a big black snake
A hum, a hum

15 So that's the end of one two three
A hum, a hum
That's the end of one two three
The Rat, the Frog and Miss Mousie
A hum, a hum

16 There's bread and cheese upon the shelf
A hum, a hum
There's bread and cheese upon the shelf
If you want any more just sing it yourself
A hum, a hum

# The Girl I've Left Behind Me

Traditional

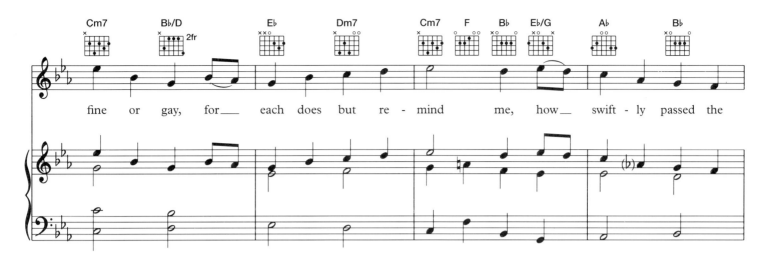

fine or gay, for___ each does but re - mind me, how___ swift - ly passed the

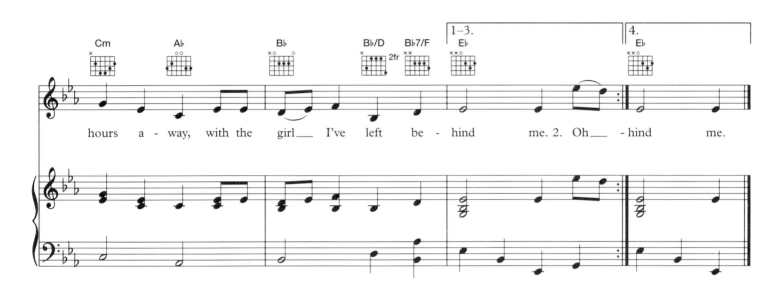

hours a - way, with the girl___ I've left be - hind me. 2. Oh___ -hind me.

2 Oh, ne'er shall I forget the night
The stars were bright above me
And gently lent their silvery light
When first she vowed to love me!
But now I'm bound to Brighton camp
Kind heaven then pray guide me
And send me safely back again
To the girl I've left behind me

3 Her golden hair in ringlets fair
Her eyes like diamonds shining
Her slender waist with carriage chaste
May leave the swan repining
Ye gods above oh, hear my prayer
To my beauteous fair to bind me
And send me safely back again
To the girl I've left behind me

4 The bee shall honey taste no more
The dove become a ranger
The falling waters cease to roar
Ere I shall seek to change her
The vows we registered above
Shall ever cheer and bind me
In constancy to her I love
The girl I've left behind me

# Greensleeves

Traditional

Refrain

2  I have been ready at your hand
   To grant whatever you would crave
   I have both wagered life and land
   Your love and good will for to have
      *Greensleeves was my delight*
      *Greensleeves was my heart of gold*
      *Greensleeves was my lady love*
      *And who but my lady Greensleeves*

3  I bought thee kerchiefs to thy head
   That were wrought fine and gallantly
   I kept thee both at board and bed
   Which cost my purse well favoredly
      *Greensleeves was my . . .*

4  Thy smock of gold so crimson red
   With pearls bedecked sumptously
   The like no other lasses had
   And yet thou wouldest not love me
      *Greensleeves was my . . .*

5  Thy gown was of the grassy green
   Thy sleeves of satin hanging by
   Which made thee be our harvest queen
   And yet thou wouldest not love me
      *Greensleeves was my . . .*

6  Thou couldst desire no earthly thing
   But still thou hadst it readily
   Thy music still to play and sing
   And yet thou wouldest not love me
      *Greensleeves was my . . .*

7  Well I will pray to God on high
   That thou my constancy mayst see
   And that yet once before I die
   Thou wilt vouchsafe to love me
      *Greensleeves was my . . .*

8  Greensleeves, now farewell, adieu!
   God I pray to prosper thee
   For I am still thy lover true
   Come once again and love me
      *Greensleeves was my . . .*

# John Peel

By John Woodcock Graves

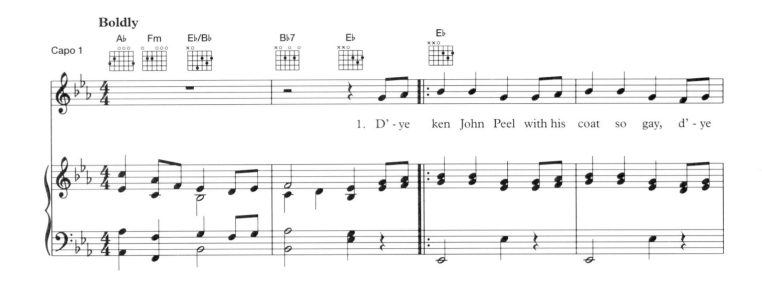

1. D'-ye ken John Peel with his coat so gay, d'-ye

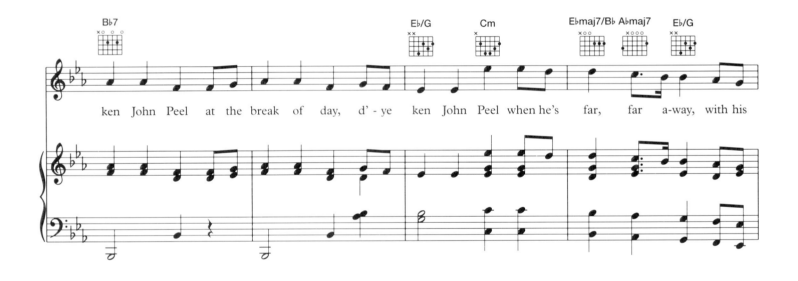

ken John Peel at the break of day, d'-ye ken John Peel when he's far, far a-way, with his

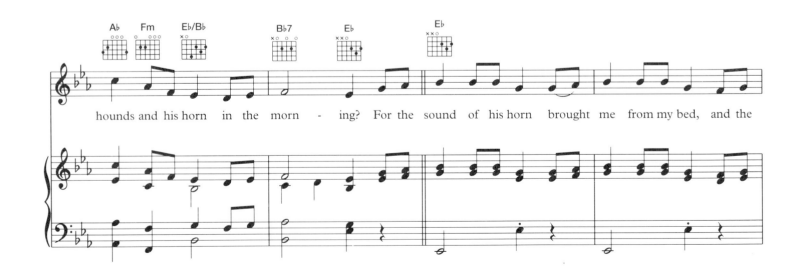

hounds and his horn in the morn - ing? For the sound of his horn brought me from my bed, and the

2   Yes I ken John Peel and Ruby too
    Ranter and Ringwood, Bellman and True
    From a find to a check, from a check to a view
    From a view to a death in the morning
        *For the sound of his horn brought me from my bed*
        *And the cry of the hounds which he oft-times led*
        *Peel's 'View halloo!' would awaken the dead*
        *Or the fox from his lair in the morning*

3   Then here's to John Peel from my heart and soul
    Let's drink to his health, let's finish the bowl
    We'll follow John Peel through fair and through foul
    If we want a good hunt in the morning
        *For the sound of his horn . . .*

4   D'ye ken John Peel with his coat so gay?
    He lived at Troutbeck once on a day
    Now he has gone far, far, far away
    We shall ne'er hear his voice in the morning
        *For the sound of his horn . . .*

# Johnny Todd

Traditional

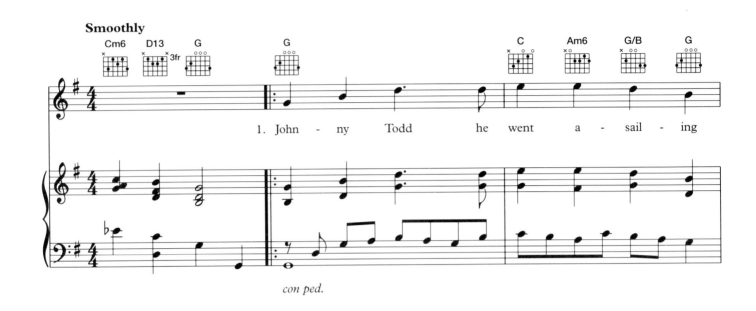

1. John - ny Todd he went a - sail - ing

for to cross the o - cean wide, but he left

his true love be - hind him walk - ing by the

Li - ver - pool  tide.     - fore  you  go.

2   For a week she wept full sorely
    Tore her hair and wrung her hands
    Till she met with another sailor
    Walking on the Liverpool sands

3   Oh fair maid why are you weeping
    For your Johnny gone to sea?
    If you'll wed with me tomorrow
    I will kind and constant be

4   I will buy you sheets and blankets
    I'll buy you a wedding ring
    You shall have a silver cradle
    For to rock the baby in

5   Johnny Todd came home from sailing
    Sailing o'er the ocean wide
    But he found that his fair and false one
    Was another sailor's bride

6   Now young men who go a-sailing
    For to fight the foreign foe
    Do not leave your love like Johnny
    Marry her before you go

# The Lass Of Richmond Hill

Words and Music by
Leonard MacNally and James Hook

# The Lincolnshire Poacher

Traditional

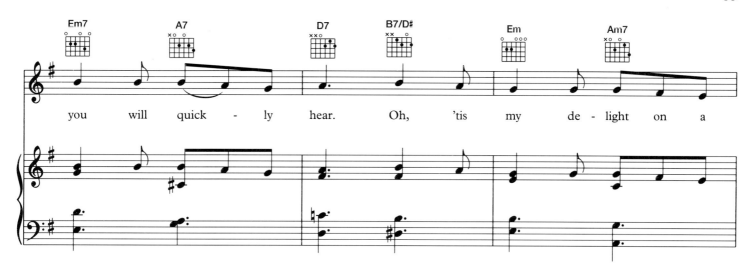

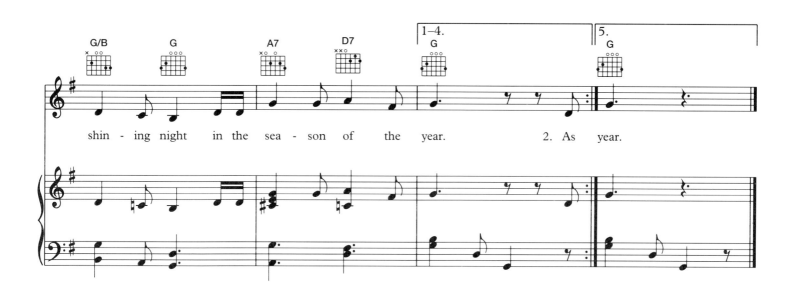

2 As me and my companions
  Were setting on a snare
  'Twas when we spied the gamekeeper
  For him we did not care
  For we can wrestle and fight, my boys
  And jump out anywhere
    *Oh 'tis my delight*
    *On a shining night*
    *In the season of the year*

3 As me and my companions
  Were setting four and five
  And taking on 'em up again
  We caught a hare alive
  We took a hare alive, my boys
  And through the wood did steer
    *Oh 'tis my . . .*

4 I threw him on my shoulder
  And then we trudged home
  We took him to a neighbour's house
  And sold him for a crown
  We sold him for a crown, my boys
  But I did not tell you where
    *Oh 'tis my . . .*

5 Success to every gentleman
  That lives in Lincolnshire
  Success to every poacher
  That wants to sell a hare
  Bad luck to every gamekeeper
  That will not sell his deer
    *Oh 'tis my . . .*

# On Ilkley Moor Baht 'At

Traditional

**Firmly and with gusto**

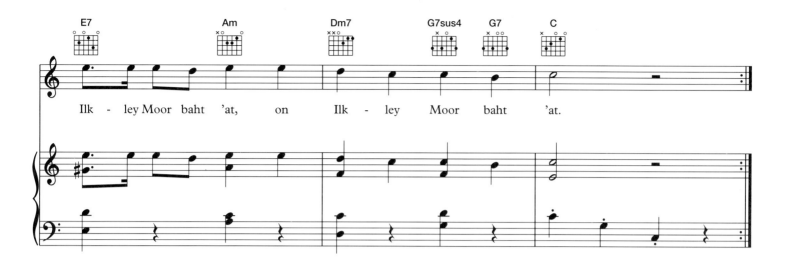

Ilk - ley Moor baht 'at, on Ilk - ley Moor baht 'at.

2  I've been a-courting Mary Jane
On Ilkley Moor baht 'at
I've been a-courting Mary Jane
I've been a-courting Mary Jane
    *On Ilkley Moor baht 'at*
    *On Ilkley Moor baht 'at*
    *On Ilkley Moor baht 'at*

3  Thou'll surely catch thy death of cold
On Ilkley Moor baht 'at
Thou'll surely catch thy death of cold
Thou'll surely catch thy death of cold
    *On Ilkley Moor . . .*

4  Then we shall have to bury thee
On Ilkley Moor baht 'at
Then we shall have to bury thee
Then we shall have to bury thee
    *On Ilkley Moor . . .*

5  Then worms will come and eat thee oop
On Ilkley Moor baht 'at
Then worms will come and eat thee oop
Then worms will come and eat thee oop
    *On Ilkley Moor . . .*

6  Then dooks will come and eat oop worms
On Ilkley Moor baht 'at
Then dooks will come and eat oop worms
Then dooks will come and eat oop worms
    *On Ilkley Moor . . .*

7  Then we will come and eat oop ducks
On Ilkley Moor baht 'at
Then we will come and eat oop ducks
Then we will come and eat oop ducks
    *On Ilkley Moor . . .*

8  Then we will have thee back again
On Ilkley Moor baht 'at
Then we will have thee back again
Then we will have thee back again
    *On Ilkley Moor . . .*

# Scarborough Fair

Traditional

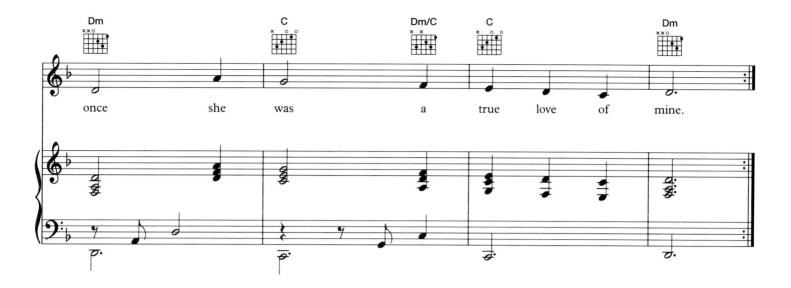

once      she   was      a    true   love   of    mine.

2   Tell her to make me a cambric shirt
    (*Parsley sage rosemary and thyme*)
    Without any seam or fine needlework
    For once she was a true love of mine.

3   Tell her to wash it in yonder dry well
    (*Parsley sage rosemary and thyme*)
    Where water ne'er sprung, nor drop of rain fell
    For once she was a true love of mine

4   Tell her to dry it on yonder thorn
    (*Parsley sage rosemary and thyme*)
    Which never bore blossom since Adam was born
    For once she was a true love of mine

5   Will you find me an acre of land
    (*Parsley sage rosemary and thyme*)
    Between the sea foam and the sea sand?
    For once she was a true love of mine

6   Will you plough it with a lamb's horn
    (*Parsley sage rosemary and thyme*)
    And sow it all over with one peppercorn?
    For once she was a true love of mine

7   Will you reap it with sickle of leather
    (*Parsley sage rosemary and thyme*)
    And tie it all up with a peacock's feather?
    For once she was a true love of mine

8   When you've done and finished your work
    (*Parsley sage rosemary and thyme*)
    Then come to me for your cambric shirt
    And you shall be a true love of mine

# Tobacco's But An Indian Weed

Traditional

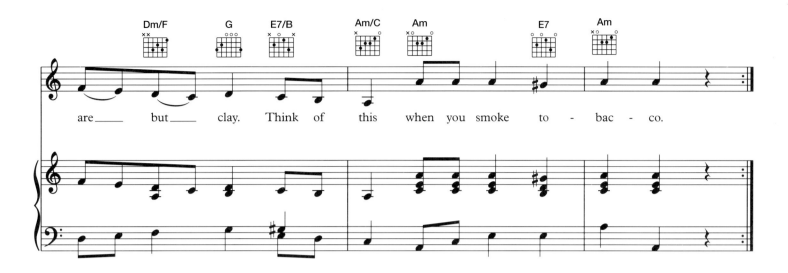

are ____ but ____ clay. Think of this when you smoke to - bac - co.

2    The pipe that is so lilywhite
      Wherein so many take delight
      Gone with a touch
      Man's life is such
      Think on this when you smoke tobacco

3    The pipe that is so foul within
      Shows how the soul is stained with sin
      It doth require
      The purging fire
      Think on this when you smoke tobacco

4    The ashes that are left behind
      Do serve to put us all in mind
      That unto dust
      Return we must
      Think on this when you smoke tobacco

5    The smoke that doth so high ascend
      Shows that our life must have an end
      The vapour's gone
      Man's life is done
      Think on this when you smoke tobacco

# The Vicar Of Bray

Traditional

**With firmness**

I'll main-tain, un-til my dy-ing day sir, that what-so-ev-er king may reign, still I'll be the vi-car of Bray, sir. 2. When Bray, sir.

2  When Royal James possessed the crown
   And Popery came in fashion
   The Penal Laws I hooted down
   And read the Declaration
   The Church of Rome I found did fit
   Full well my constitution
   And I had been a Jesuit
   But for the Revolution
        *And this is law that I'll maintain*
        *Until my dying day, sir*
        *That whatsoever king may reign*
        *I'll be the vicar of Bray, sir*

3  When William was our King declared
   To ease the nation's grievance
   With this new wind about I steered
   And swore to him allegiance
   Old principles I did revoke
   Set conscience at a distance
   Passive obedience was a joke
   A jest was non-resistance
        *And this is law . . .*

4  When Royal Anne became our queen
   The Church of England's glory
   Another face of things was seen
   And I became a Tory
   Occasional Conformists base
   I blamed their moderation
   And thought the Church in danger was
   By such prevarication
        *And this is law . . .*

5  When George in pudding time came o'er
   And moderate men looked big, sir
   My principles I changed once more
   And so became a Whig, sir
   And thus preferment I procured
   From our new faith's defender
   And almost every day adjured
   The Pope and the Pretender
        *And this is law . . .*

6  The illustrious house of Hanover
   And Protestant succession
   To these I do allegiance swear
   While they can keep possession
   For in my faith and loyalty
   I never more will falter
   And George my lawful king shall be
   Until the times do alter
        *And this is law . . .*

# Villikins And His Dinah

Traditional

**Heartily**

1. It is of a rich mer - chant I am go - ing for to tell, who had for a daugh - ter an un- com-mon nice young gal. Her name it was Di - nah, just six - teen years

2  As Dinah was a-walking her garden one day
   Her papa he came to her, and thus he did say
   'Go dress yourself Dinah in gorgeous array
   And get you a husband both gallant and gay!'
       *Singin', too-ra-li too-ra-li too-ra-li day*

3  'Oh papa, oh papa, I've not made up my mind
   And to marry just yet why, I don't feel inclined
   To you my large fortune I'll gladly give o'er
   If you'll let me live single a year or two more'
       *Singin', too-ra-li . . .*

4  'Go, go boldest daughter' the parent replied
   'If you won't consent to be this here young man's bride
   I'll give your large fortune to the nearest of kin
   And you shan't reap the benefit of one single pin'
       *Singin', too-ra-li . . .*

5  As Villikins was walking the garden around
   He spied his dear Dinah lying dead on the ground
   And a cup of cold pizen it lay by her side
   With a billet-doux stating 'twas by pizen she died
       *Singin', too-ra-li . . .*

6  He kissed her cold corpus a thousand times o'er
   And called her his Dinah though she was no more
   Then swallowed the pizen like a lover so brave
   And Villikins and his Dinah lie both in one grave
       *Singin', too-ra-li . . .*

7  Now all you young maidens take warning by her
   Never not by no means disobey your governor
   And all you young fellows mind who you clap eyes on
   Think of Villikins and Dinah and the cup of cold pizen
       *Singin', too-ra-li . . .*

# What Shall We Do With The Drunken Sailor?

Traditional

**Boldly**

1. What shall we do with the drunk - en sail - or?

What shall we do with the drunk - en sail - or? What shall we do with the drunk - en sail - or

ear - lye in the morn - ing? Hoo - ray and up she ris - es, hoo - ray and

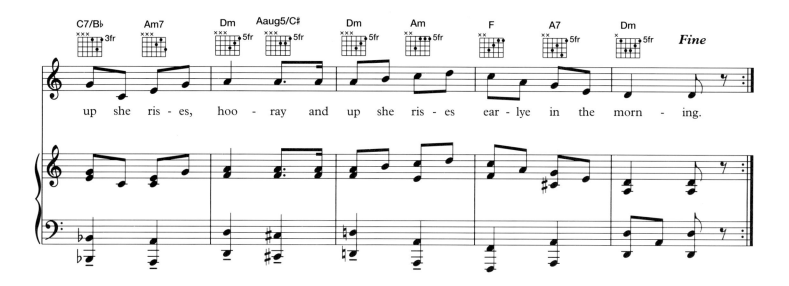

up she ris - es, hoo - ray and up she ris - es ear - lye in the morn - ing.

*Fine*

2   Put him in a long boat till he's sober
    Put him in a long boat till he's sober
    Put him in a long boat till he's sober
    Earlye in the morning
        *Hooray and up she rises*
        *Hooray and up she rises*
        *Hooray and up she rises*
        *Earlye in the morning*

3   Hang him by the leg in a running bowline
    Hang him by the leg in a running bowline
    Hang him by the leg in a running bowline
    Earlye in the morning
        *Hooray and up . . .*

4   Put him in the scuppers with a hose pipe on him
    Put him in the scuppers with a hose pipe on him
    Put him in the scuppers with a hose pipe on him
    Earlye in the morning
        *Hooray and up . . .*

5   Shave his belly with a rusty razor
    Shave his belly with a rusty razor
    Shave his belly with a rusty razor
    Earlye in the morning
        *Hooray and up . . .*

6   That's what we'll do with the drunken sailor
    That's what we'll do with the drunken sailor
    That's what we'll do with the drunken sailor
    Earlye in the morning
        *Hooray and up . . .*

# The Wraggle-Taggle Gypsies

Traditional

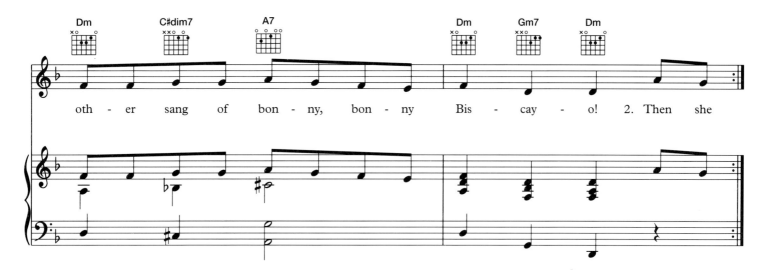

oth - er sang of bon - ny, bon - ny Bis - cay - o! 2. Then she

2    Then she pulled off her silk-finished gown
      And put on hose of leather-o
      The ragged, ragged rags about our door
      And she's gone with the wraggle-taggle gypsies-o!

3    It was last night when my lord came home
      Inquiring for his a-lady-o
      The servants said on every hand
      She's gone with the wraggle-taggle gypsies-o!

4    Oh, saddle to me my milk-white steed,
      And go fetch me my pony-o!
      That I may ride and seek my bride
      Who is gone with the wraggle-taggle gypsies-o

5    Oh, he rode high and he rode low
      He rode through woods and copses-o
      Until he came to a wide open field
      A-there he espied his a-lady-o

6    What makes you leave your house and land?
      What makes you leave your money-o?
      What makes you leave your new-wedded lord
      To go with the wraggle-taggle gypsies-o?

7    What care I for my house and land?
      What care I for money-o?
      What care I for my new-wedded lord?
      I'm off with the wraggle-taggle gypsies-o!

8    Last night you slept on a goose-feather bed
      With the sheet turned down so bravely-o!
      Tonight you'll sleep in a cold open field
      Along with the wraggle-taggle gypsies-o!

9    What care I for a goose-feather bed
      With the sheet turned down so bravely-o?
      For tonight I shall sleep in a cold open field
      Along with the wraggle-taggle gypsies-o!

Printed in England
Panda Press · Haverhill · Suffolk · 7/95